The Racial, Moral, and Ethical Considerations for Abortions: Autonomy & Sentient Morality

There ought to be more discussions of the things that matter, on the things that drive us apart, and that which we are uncomfortable talking about. If there were, we would be accustomed to being challenged and refuted and being more understanding towards others. *The Racial, Moral, and Ethical Considerations for Abortion* looks at how we think about abortion. Why our thinking is flawed and seeks to point out inconsistencies in our thoughts and beliefs. This book strives to be scientifically accurate, but without the distractions of scientific vocabulary and jargon. Instead, we will focus our minds and think, examine our beliefs, and answer the hard questions. Are abortions cruel? Are they merciful or just? Are they necessary to preserve and protect our most vulnerable? What does it mean to kill, is it wrong, and can it ever be justified? Furthermore, why do we believe the things we do? Why is it that some proponents of abortion support the birth of a child, but also wish that government spending not be wasted on these mothers? We will talk about motherhood, its pains, its tribulations, as well as discuss single motherhood, race, and poverty. When answering these questions this book will hold nothing back.

Table of Contents

Introduction ---6

Chapter 1: Common Arguments for and Against Abortions-------------11

Chapter 2: Analysis of Argument in Favor of Abortion------------------17

Chapter 3: Argument Against Abortion-------------------------------------27

Chapter 4: Why Religious Justification Fails-----------------------------30

Chapter 5: Abortions Should Not Be Centered Only Around the Baby--39

Chapter 6: The Multifaceted Risks of Pregnancies----------------------44

Chapter 7: Redefining the Morality of Murder---------------------------50

Chapter 8: Sentience & Morality---58

Chapter 9: Late-Term Abortions, Can They Ever be Justified? ---------64

Chapter 10: Ethics and More--- 71

Chapter 11: Combining Morality, Ethics, and Law---------------------- 74

Chapter 12: Liberties and the Practical Implications of Abortions------ 80

Contacting The Author--- 87

References---89

Introduction

In this book I hope to present a new way of thinking of not just abortions, but of people, animals, and moral thought altogether. This book and I do not take a scientific approach to this issue, an emphasis on the scientific details would not add much onto this discussion and would distract us from the true focus of this book: the morality of abortions and their subsequent implications. This book is meant to be more philosophic than scientific in nature, but aims to be scientifically correct, when necessary, except with the use of the word "baby" and "early-term" and "late-term" abortions. For the sake of being clear, concise, and uniform throughout this book, you should understand that the word "baby" when in quotes refers to the fertilized egg, or embryo at any time while it is in the womb, and that without it refers to the actual birthed baby. Secondly, the scientific data is inconclusive about when a baby can feel sensations of pain, but it is generally agreed upon that by 20 weeks (about 4 and a half months) they most definitely feel pain. Therefore, let us assume for now that early-term refers to 20 weeks of pregnancy and before, and late-term refers to more than 20 weeks. After much consideration I find myself in support of early-term abortions, but I remain skeptical on the morality of late-term abortions. Nonetheless, I do believe there are times in which a late-term abortion could be justified.

The goal of this book is to demonstrate a clear, consistent, and systematic thought process. What I mean by this is that if we believe, for example, killing in one instance is to be justified, then it ought to be justified in other similar situations. If you believe in the pro-life movement but support the death penalty these views are contradictory. How can you morally justify the killing of an unarmed harmless person who has already been deprived of his liberties, and has been detained by the state; and then sport the notion that life should always be preserved at all costs? It should be entirely possible to hold these two views simultaneously, but not for the reason mentioned prior. Even if a person were to formulate some way for these two views to be held simultaneously with the reason prior, most people would not have done so before this reading; and this is what I believe to be a problem for much of America. As there are a great many of people who would protest and advocate in support of the continuation of the death penalty and the discontinuation of abortions, yet they have not even considered much larger contradictions than the one presented here.

We are citizens who exist in a democratic society, and with social media and information technology we hold more power than ever, yet the proofs for our beliefs get lazier and lazier. Which is why I author this book also for myself, as my way of proving I put time, effort, and that I care about the things that I believe in, and that I did not just lazily follow along with what I had been taught when growing up. You do not need to author a book to prove this, but you do need to think and challenge yourself. This leads to my second goal of this book, to propose what I believe to be a solid and concise answer and theory to the moral dilemma of abortion and its own implications.

We often take many of our beliefs for granted, rarely ever challenging them, we are so sure of them that we rarely ever think twice about their validity, and when we do, we dismiss anything contradicting them as hubris. Human thought and morality, especially those amongst the masses, fall under extraordinarily little scrutiny. The reason for this, is surely overly complex, but to simplify; it is due to the failure to adopt a systematic approach to our moral judgements, and thus a lack of consistency. As humans, no, as sentient beings we tend to put faith in our mental abilities and thought processes, however, this is a false sense of pride and security. If everyone, and I can assure many people do, had the utmost conviction in their own beliefs and this alone sufficed as proof of their validity, then there could be no progress. We must carefully, and thoroughly examine our own beliefs, our morals, and the arguments we present for them being true. To do anything otherwise is a great disservice to our community, our country, and those around us.

It is unthinkable to believe that one's untrained strength of reason be anywhere comparable to that of someone who frequently and systematically practices and applies their own reason to the world. For this reason, I deeply employ the readers of both trained and untrained mind alike to think beyond just mere surface level feelings and intuition, to challenge and argue against the things they believe in, and to not just accept or dismiss any argument with your own unexamined feelings but by actively trying to strike down each of my claims, as well as your own. Ask yourself, "why do I feel this? Does this make sense? Is this consistent with other values and ideals I hold dear?" It is your own duty, as the master of your own mind. If our world were to operate on the mere whims of what we felt to be right at whatever given moment, many would, and surely have, suffered.

Let me be clear, no person, no matter how capable they believe themselves to be, will ever be competent enough to reliably make moral judgements without having been formally taught, having challenged themselves, having been challenged by others, or having developed a systematic approach to rational and consistent thought, or what can be summarized as critical thinking and analysis. Furthermore, even if they were to have developed these analytical and critical thinking skills their arguments may be imperfect. Otherwise, there would be no debate, no controversy, and surely this book need not be created, but here we are.

Chapter 1: Common Arguments for and Against Abortion

Let us call into account the primary issue at hand, abortions, and their common arguments in favor and against. The ideas expressed in this chapter and the next are not necessarily of my own, but what I believe to be a brief overview of the most common arguments that I am aware of.

The first of which is a woman's (reproductive) rights, and that a woman has the right to their own body along with its maintenance, use, and the sensations that it allows her. The result of which is the ability to terminate pregnancy of the fetus so that she can maintain this right. If we were, for example, to touch a woman, she would reserve the right to terminate further contact because she remains in control, or autonomous, over her own body, likewise the same applies to the "baby," which occupies a much more burdensome load on the body and mind than any normal form of physical contact.

Another argument in favor of abortion is that the birth of a child would result in a miserable life of the child, and/or mother, and that the birth of the child would be unfortunate and sorrowful, and so it would be better off not having been born as its birth would only cause more suffering. This approach focuses on the practical implications of giving birth, but also appeals to the morality of giving birth to what proponents assume will be a miserable life for the child and parents.

Other arguments stem to include the unfair continued preservation of a system that represses marginalized groups, such as woman, people of color, and the combination of the two. Women usually are forced to give up their aspirations in life to mother a child and are thus further excluded from higher positions, economic equality, and education. Studies show that regardless of whether it is a man or woman who decides to take care of the child, wages seem to drop significantly, although, even more so if it is a man who decides to care of the child. The most surprising part of this study, which was conducted by Chicago University, is that if you exclude mothers from the equation, women make 96% of what men make, almost completely destroying the wage gap when compared to the 80% when including mothers (Hassenfeld & Vander Ploeg, 2018). Likewise, for people of color, supporting a child, either through legal child support, or through parenting, bears an acute financial and chronic burden on the parents, which, if we are talking about people of color, will prove to be far more detrimental and thus leading to further poverty of both the parents, and future generations.

Arguments *against* abortion tend to vary. Some of their proponents primarily make use of religious justifications for abortions using ideas and facts assumed to be true by their religion. Other arguments focus on morality and the rational justification, or rather, the lack thereof for abortions. There are also some legal debates that look at Roe Vs. Wade, but we will not delve into these too much. The strongest arguments emphasize the morality and ethics of causing harm to another life. These serve as the figurative spearheads for much of the pro-life supporters and their attacks on abortion including Roe Vs. Wade. It is almost impossible to justify an abortion without first addressing the moral implications of harming the unborn child and these will be the primary interest of this book.

I think it should suffice to say that the religious arguments are quite self-explanatory. They fall under one of three categories.

Religions either explicitly deny abortions, or they are interpreted and implied that they are to shy away from abortions, or their cultural groups, which are impacted by a common religion, traditionally stay away from abortions without explicit or implicit commands to do so.

Some of the common arguments, fall under what I call a prima facie obligation to deny an abortion, and to preserve life. This means they view life as something that ought to be prioritized and that there are no reasons to think about challenging this. Whatever situation holds the greatest net amount of life, is the correct situation because life is intrinsically valuable. It holds life to be a sacred and holy gift bestowed by God, and that killing is a sin and that the answer to abortions is obvious. Their arguments fall under, killing being sinful, preservation of life, and similar things of this nature. These are distinct from people who use religion as auxiliary support to their argument against abortions, or to those who use religion exclusively against other devout members of their religion and not against others who do not believe. They justify their reasonings through religion first, and then whatever auxiliary facts they have, are second. Due to their arguments being routed in religion it leads to obvious problems, and I will discuss these in depth later. However, they also possess an inherent advantage when playing on the home field. That is, when convincing other members of their religious congregation or community that abortions are wrong; their arguments are even more effective. They have a predetermined and established set of absolute rules set forth by their religion and use it as a guideline for correct behavior, however this strength is less effective when they try to argue with increasingly secular populations.

Outside of the religious appeal, support for pro-life focuses on a moral appeal backed by evidence that fetuses can feel pain. It is immoral to cause harm to another human being, and this makes for a sturdy argument against abortions, or a strong auxiliary argument when religion is the primary means of argumentation. Their argument's strength is derived from morality and the portrayal of the "baby" as an equal human being. What makes this form of pro-life distinct from the religious one is that their arguments do not emphasize religion as an important reason, although they may mention it.

There are also other arguments that should be acknowledged such as arguments against the decision of Roe Vs. Wade. They argue that the supreme court's decision to uphold woman's privacy is obsolete because there is no right to privacy guaranteed by the constitution. Another argument is that abortions make human life seem more disposable, and that this presents an ethical dilemma. I think the most interesting of the lesser-known arguments is that modern day abortion is the "modern-day equivalent of Eugenics" (Anderson, 2015).

Chapter 2: Analysis of Arguments in Favor of Abortion

Firstly, regardless of whether you are for or against abortion, we are all in favor of humanity, for in this, there are no sides to take, except our own. We are all hoping that our views are right, and that they are implemented into law so that we can make humanity better. None of us propose arguments simply to spite one another, however, this does not mean we must not evaluate all claims with the utmost scrutiny.

Most arguments in favor of abortions are logically derived, there seems to be some logical and moral truth hidden in all of these, but individually they are lacking. They also fail to address and specifically counter the opinions of some of those across the aisle. Specifically, religion, but to a lesser extent the morality of killing a "baby". Although in all fairness, it remains quite difficult to argue against religion. However, I will touch upon religion and its implications within my own thoughts later. It is also worth noting that the nature of these argument must be more logical. If we were to justify the murder of a man, our justification to legalize the murder, should be nothing less than logical, and that it was necessary for the benefit of humanity, another's self-defense, or one's own self-preservation. Otherwise, I would be considered having faulty morals, bad judgement, or to have gone against the laws, and the ethics that guide us. When assessing whether a person is guilty of a crime, we only care if they meet the criteria of that crime. We do not stop to think about whether a person has family, whether they grew up poor and unlucky, or whatever contingent factors that may arise; we only care if they did it. Similarly, proponents of abortion must defend the murder of the "baby" with the same amount of rigor. They must argue that it is not murder but self-defense or some other concept.

One argument I find remarkably interesting, is one that assumes a child will suffer because they were born impoverished, with parents who claim that they are not responsible or capable of parenting at the time of pregnancy. They may also claim that there may be some unfortunate circumstance and that it would better to end the suffering early or prevent it entirely. We often assume that regardless of circumstance, life is the greatest gift, and this argument strives to partially strike this assumption down. This argument, while making sense, is contradictory by itself. If we are to say that it would be better to not give birth because of faulty circumstances, then that means we are assuming the baby will suffer. However, suffering is relative and subjective. It would be improper to say a poor family in New York, or California is suffering simply because they are impoverished. The child may escape poverty, or even live a content life while being impoverished. Moreover, babies cannot understand the social construct of poverty. Additionally, how can a child who knows nothing but poverty, and has adapted to that poverty suffer, when he has never experienced anything but poverty. In this case, why do we not weep and cry for the kings and queens of past, they must have had a tough time living in luxurious palaces without air conditioning and modern technology. Or the smaller nomadic tribes that live their life happily without modern technology and a dollar to their name. We understand why. They have never had technology, so they were never capable of feeling feelings of suffering or suffering out of want for these things. To suffer from the absence of something, means that something must have first been there to begin with.

  The true reason we propose this argument is not because the child will suffer from poverty, but rather, it is because the parents will suffer from watching their own child be impoverished and suffer more from the pain because they too will suffer from being further impoverished, and then once more because they guilt of not being able to provide the common amenities that other children are portrayed to have in the media.

One could argue that the child suffers in the absence of something he has never had because he sees others with them and becomes envious. This is a fair refutation of the previous statements, and one that highlights an equally alarming problem on the pro-life side. That is, their inconsistency in their "pro-life" ideals. It is safe to say that a great many of people who do not believe in abortions live in rural areas, are traditional, conservative, or are Republican. However, these groups tend to also be against government welfare designed to help these children and mothers, and what they call "socialist" programs. They only care that the baby is born, and once it is born, they do not care what happens to it any longer. If they did care, they would also strive to support the mothers and households, advocate for government intervention to help them financially, rather than government intervention into the bodies of a stranger they will soon forget, abandon, and then criticize. It is fine to argue and advocate for the banning of abortions, but if you are to do so, you ought to try and take responsibility for the diminished quality of life that is a direct result of the ban. Comparatively, feeding wild animals, while born out of empathy and good intentions, is bad. They become increasingly reliant on the person feeding them, such that the moment you let go of their hand they fail to adapt and die. Proponents of "pro-life" are feeding mothers, they are trying to forcefully change the environment of their peers and they either will not or cannot offer the resources necessary to help the parents and the child thrive. These are the inconsistencies in our thoughts and beliefs that we ought to correct, if you must believe that abortions are wrong, these are answers and problems that must be answered; rather than following along the political ideals and jargon that label these mothers, communities, and children as, "ghettos" "criminals" "free-loaders," and similar insults. If you insist abortions should not be, then you must take responsibility for the lives it will affect.

There is an even deeper argument to be found here. It is reasonable to conclude that regardless of which part of the United

States you live in, you are likely to be much better off than a significantly less developed country. In this case, do we argue that abortions are wrong, and that this argument is invalid because abortions are simply immoral and life too precious; or do we argue that this argument is invalid only because the U.S is fortunate enough for even its poorest children to live decent lives when compared to the worst parts of the world? If you say the latter, then that ought to mean abortions should be justified elsewhere, and if you say the former, then the immorality of abortions is absolute. There are places, or at the very least have been places, where the suffering of a child has commonly been much greater than any benefit of life. I would even argue that without the freedom, dignity, and prosperity that is commonly found in America, life may not even be worth living. Without at least one of these three aspects of life present how sure are that life is worth living: even in the worst places? The reason this is relevant is to establish whether you honestly believe the preservation of life; no matter how miserable, degrading, and painful it may be, will always be worth living. Once you believe there is even a single instance in which abortion ought to be legal, subsequent holes begin to appear, and eventually all sorts of exceptions persist, and you must reassess your beliefs.

Personally, I find the argument that marginalized groups would suffer the most from 'pro-life' to be more convincing, especially when combined with the argument prior. Although the birth rates for black women have begun to align with white women over the past several decades, it remains true that historically, black women have had significantly higher birth rates than that of white women. Additionally, despite having ***significantly*** higher abortion rates, the birth rates of black women remain slightly higher than white women. In 2010, the birth rates were 57.3, 61.3, and 65.4 for whites, blacks, and Hispanics per one thousand births respectively (Livingston, 2012). While blacks and Hispanics have significantly higher birth rates child-rearing is a financially intensive burden, one that white women are likely to afford more readily, and one that blacks cannot. Poverty and birth rates tend to correlate strongly with one another, and whether its poverty causing high birth rates, or high birth rates causing poverty, neither spell good for people of color (Schultz, 2005). However, it is also worth noting that it is the less privileged minorities using these services. Data dating back to 2005 shows that the pregnancy rate per 1000 women, *which should not be confused with birth rate,* were at 123 and 125 for black and Hispanic people; it was only 43 for white women. The abortion rate was 26, 62, and 82 respectively for white black and Hispanics (Guttmacher Institute, 2010). Does this mean brown people would be even more impoverished if not for abortions? Plagued by single parent households, poor education, less job opportunities than there are already, as well as low income living and an intense need for low-income housing; I believe we would have had a much bigger issue to address if not for Roe vs Wade. The data implies that without abortions both poor families and communities would remain impoverished almost indefinitely and far more severely.

These facts show that abortion may have saved much of the U.S from what might have been a disastrous human rights issue that would have plagued a large amount of black and brown communities. While the common arguments regarding the reduction of unhappy or under privileged babies in the world seems to be lacking individually, when taken together with the argument of racial equality it becomes sound. Stretching this hypothetical even further, I am also certain it would be these under privileged communities that would have been hit hardest during the recent COVID-19 pandemic. Poor living conditions, higher population density, and a small supply of available and affordable homes would have resulted in scenes comparable to the advertisements asking us to donate to foreign countries in need. Food, health, environment, and clean energy are big enough issues as is with the current population, but without abortions one can only imagine what we would do with millions more in our population. Yet, these questions have never been asked or answered, indicating that politicians and proponents of pro-life have even begun to scratch surface of the problem they are trying to create.

There is another smaller argument within the one prior that can also be made, that is, that amongst those who are against abortions many of them live in states where land is cheaper, and the cost of living is also cheaper. They are likely to be white and more privileged. While some of this generalization of characteristics is anecdotal, the fact remains that the amount of land available correlates with fertility. If a family has more land, they are also more likely to have a child (Schultz, 2005). Additionally, busier, more independent women have lower fertility rates because their time is more "valuable," women simply do not have as much time on their hand when they are independent and working, and to force women away from this independency to stay in the kitchen and raise children is another problem altogether.

Fertility rates are not as simple as, "poor people have more children, and the rich do not". It is affected by several variables, many in favor and against. For example, fertility rates tend to spike because of sudden increases in income (Black, 2013). This means that in select cases, sudden increases to income or even housing prices may suddenly raise fertility rates. However, it remains that there is a strong correlation between poverty and fertility is profoundly strong (Lovenheim, 2013). Culture, religion, location, wealth, and sudden increases to wealth are just some of the impacts in fertility rates.

Chapter 3: Arguments Against Abortion

A lot of the arguments against abortion are either religious or moral, and we can categorize most of them as such. For example, many people hold the position that abortion is morally wrong because we are 'killing babies.' This is a misconception, as they are not yet babies. When we consider the morality of abortions, we need to look at how far along the pregnancy is. Are we a few weeks, a few months, six months? Depending on your answer you may have different views, but surely, we can say that in the extremely early days of a pregnancy the "baby" is not much different than any other part of the body. It would be rather unusual if we say that they are babies, they most certainly are not. Proponents on this side of the aisle need to consider when the "baby" feels pain, whether it can be avoided, and whether this pain ought to override the plight of its mother. Research looking into whether fetuses can feel pain is of particular interest, and we should also consider these. When we examine morality or ethics there are a few principles we are to abide by. One is to avoid killing if possible. Second, is to reduce pain and suffering as much as possible. Third, is to withhold from unjustified, cruel, or unusual punishments and to hold people accountable for their wrong actions. These things conflict regardless of what said of the argument you are on.

If you are pro-abortion, you may be inflicting pain, suffering, and inducing death. However, if you are against abortion the pregnancy causes pain and suffering for the mother, and it is difficult to say the mother has done a punishable crime and should thus be forced to carry out the punishment of giving birth. We ought to stay consistent and systematic in our thought processes. We say, "all men are born equal," at least in terms of value under the law. Although the "baby" has yet to be born, we are valuing it as more valuable than the mother. So much so that we would expect the mother to sacrifice her livelihood after having done nothing legally or morally wrong. You might be wondering, when can a baby feel pain? The answer is prone to some debate, but fetuses definitely develop the ability to sense pain at around 24 weeks (about 5 and a half months), there is plenty consensus that it can feel pain at 20 weeks (about 4 and a half months) and even 18 weeks (about 4 months), and some research indicates as little as 12 weeks (about 3 months), and estimates on the very bottom of this spectrum say 8 weeks (about 2 months) (Derbyshire. 2019). However, more importantly is the degree of pain they can feel, if it is reasonable or unreasonable, and whether the mother even be responsible for the "baby's" pain to begin with. These are, to me, the saddest things to consider. No one takes pleasure in having an abortion, however, there is some sigh of relief. That your life or livelihood may have been saved, that you have preserved your freedom. Like a person that calls out sick for work and that very same day the person who took their place died or became disabled. They would certainly feel sorry and mourn for them, but they would never wish to have taken his place, they would be glad it was them and not themselves. This, however, would not make you an immoral person, and no one would believe you to be immoral either; but it seems that because we are talking about an unborn child the situation changes. Suddenly, we throw all other principles we live by out the window, and some insist on forcing others to do the same. Self-preservation is an instinct, and a right that all people ought to be able to exercise. The baby is not at fault, but to say the parents are at fault for doing what their bodies and instincts urge them to do is not much better.

Chapter 4: Why Religious Justification Fails

Religion is an extremely sensitive topic, and a highly diverse and opinionated one at that. Any one wrong misstep or insensitive remark could spark outrage. Despite this, I will be utterly frank and clear in my messaging. To put it bluntly, there is no room for religion in the arguments in abortion.

For centuries, we have been strangely engrossed in the idea of religious freedom, and rightfully so. I agree that religious freedom is necessary, should be celebrated, and exercised. However, let us not forget that this is a matter of religion, that of which there are many, and that, they are not matters of fact. We, in the modern world, save a select few countries, remain civilized, organized, and church is separate from state. Religious arguments for or against religion have no place in any discussion of the moral and ethical implications of abortions.

Firstly, there is a matter of *which* religion. If we are to use religious premises, for example the Christian God to support our arguments on the topics of abortion, then why aren't we using another religion's? What makes the Christian denominations so special? Is it simply because we were born Christian and so we go with Christianity? This is nonsense, completely illogical, if you only believe in something because it was conveniently available for you to adopt at a younger age do you even really believe in it at all? How can we be sure that Christianity is the one true religion, what about Buddhism, Hinduism, even the Greek Gods? How irresponsible is it to stake the fate of an entire country on something that cannot be proven? Also, that of which, has been historically proven, to be fallible. Lest not forget that the bible is susceptible to changes, multiple editions, revisions, and that the Abrahamic religions themselves are just split off from one another. Is the bible even truly the bible anymore after so many changes? So, let us say, for example Christianity is the one true religion. What about the church then, as we have seen throughout the years the Church has denied, persecuted, and even killed people who have held different views? Take for example Galileo who proposed the Earth was not flat, or let us not forget that Christianity believes Earth to be only 6,000 years old, and what about the "Holy" crusades, and the countless denominations and practices of Christianity? Not only has it proven to be inconsistent and contradictory, but even more importantly the church, which is the central authority, has proven to be even worse, and in its past more dangerous and fatal than any other one man or nation of men has ever proven to be in history. God knows how many inconsistencies have been written or written over into the original bible, such that even if Christianity were the one true religion it still could not serve as something to base our laws upon.

We cannot use religion, and certainly not a church-like figure, to determine what is moral, and even more importantly what is ethical. Religion, particularly Christianity, has aged very poorly over the past centuries, and has proven to be a greater force for good when kept out of government. This is not to say that Christian values and influences are or have been negative. While Christianity, without a doubt, has led to many unjust sufferings, wars, murders, and corruption, that has only been when used in government or when instated as a state religion, either explicitly or implicitly. We do not do this anymore, and rightfully so, because now when we think of the church, we think of a place for good, worship, donations, charity, and as a community outreach center that only elevates a community for the better.

However, even if you disagree or resent me for these thoughts, which are mostly descriptive, factual, or historically true, you must agree with the following. There are hundreds of religions, and even then, hundreds of denominations of those religions. Which religion is the one true religion so that we may follow the true moral way? Buddhists say Buddhism, Hindus say Hinduism, Jews says Judaism, Muslims say Islam, and Christians say Christianity. Truly one massive game of "he said, she said" void of all meaning. So, let us say we adopt Islam's moral values, very well then, now everyone else is upset. If we were to use Judaism, now everyone else. You get the point. Listen carefully, if your religion cannot be established as being true, not just merely believed by the most people, but as true, rooted in fact and logic, with foundation and reliable history that establishes it as akin to fact, then it is immoral to push your own moral values on the society in which it thrives. Let me reiterate, if the basis of your moral views due to religion, you ought not to advocate for them to become law.

Let me explain why this is. There are several proponents of pro-life that believe abortion to be unholy or something of the like, and as such, vehemently persist that abortion should be outlawed. If your justification stands on religious ground, I believe this to be inherently immoral. Why? It is because all people should have the freedom of religion, and the government ought not to take the side of or against any religion or religious ideals. If we base our laws and justifications of such laws on religious grounds this is wrong. Nay, it is thrice wrong! It is wrong once because we impose our religion on others and the society in which they live. It is wrong twice because we do so while forsaking the very country that allows your religion to thrive, so that you can sneak around the civil liberties to subvert the freedoms of others. It is wrong thrice because it is impossible to prove any religion is true, and you might have lazily gone along with a religion you know that you cannot prove to be true and tried to establish it as a self-evident fact that society ought to obey; while knowing that many people will not agree with you, or because you did so for the sake of obtaining (political) power. For these three reasons, that which are, deprivation of civil liberties, forsaking the intent of the free society in which you live, purposeful, willful, or dangerous ignorance and/or going along with it for political power make the legal advocation for abortions wrong or immoral, I will explain this further.

The reader should not mistake my words as condemning religion as being immoral, it would be like saying, "guns are immoral," no, guns aren't capable of being immoral, the people using them are! Rather, it is the specific action of when a person tries to use it and fulfills two criteria. The first is when it is used as *justification for a rule or law*, second, when people *advocate for it to become a law or rules*. These two, together form the *intent* to do an immoral act, and the reason why it is immoral was mentioned previously. As for the third reason *why* it is immoral, "purposeful, willful, or dangerous ignorance and/or going along with it for political power make the legal advocation for abortions wrong or immoral," I will also clarify now. If a mother forgets her child in a car during a hot summer day, she has done something wrong, she may not have had immoral intent, but her negligence is indubitably wrong. Likewise, if she proclaims she has not done wrong whether out of true belief in this or because she wishes to avoid a prison sentence then she is still in the wrong. Likewise, if a politician lies to you, or goes along with a lie for more voters, then he too is immoral for acting merely for political power rather than the moral good of the people.

You may believe this is a stretch, an exaggeration, a manipulation of words and extremes, but it is not. Yes, the impoverished man who donates all his savings to the needy in his community may be a god sent individual, but if his justification for abortion which affects everyone, not just himself, falls along religious grounds it will be wrong. It will be blatantly immoral if he pushes for it on these grounds to affect change in society, because he knows many people do not agree with him. He cannot, without a doubt, prove his religion to be true (and thus the founding premise of his argument to be true), and he is forsaking the balance between church and state and the freedoms of religions of many. This holds true even if he only had the purest of intentions, because it does not change the fact that he knowingly deprived or tried to deprive others and his own country of the rights and liberties he himself have been afforded. The enacting of legislation or the intent to enact legislation that derives its primary argument from religion is thus an immoral act.

It is on these grounds that I dismiss all religious claims on the illegalization of abortions. Religious justifications in a society that is not a theocracy is immoral. You may enact or intend to enact such laws if you live in a theocracy such as Yemen and other middle eastern countries that follow the religion of Islam, but not in most of the western world; granted, only if we assume religious freedoms and liberties to be ethical and significant principles to uphold. Likewise, it would be immoral to try to enact legislation that is against a theocracy's religion. Religious justifications cannot be the primary reasons for our justifications in advocating for laws; however, they can serve as auxiliary methods, and in countries where liberties, laws, and cultures are not congruent with western thought it may prove to be morally permissible.

Some may argue that there is freedom of speech, and to those who say this, I agree. Indeed, you do have the freedom of speech, but that does not morally justify your actions. If I were to bully, tease, or swear at you or anyone else, it would be considered immoral, even though it is protected by my freedom of speech. What is not protected by anyone's freedom of speech is the ability to shout "fire" in a crowded movie theater when you know there is no fire. By endangering the lives of others and infringing upon their liberties you commit an immoral and illegal act. Similarly, when you forcefully propose the outlawing of abortions into law or any contentious matter that religion may weigh in on, and that you use as your primary justification, you are endangering and trying to supersede the rights of others with your own. While what you are doing may be legal, it is most certainly not moral.

Chapter 5: Abortions are not Just About the Babies. They never were.

My own position on abortion is one that is made up of moral and ethical considerations. I hope that by eliminating religion we can focus solely on morality and ethics, which we are more likely to share than religion and religious ideals. I found it necessary to eliminate religion because it served hand in hand with some peoples' moral justifications, and I found that to be deeply troubling because religion cannot be used as a common ground except with people who believe in the religion. Eliminating religion as the primary justification of any person's argument also helps to relieve them of any dogmatic shackles, and think critically, instead of repeating what they have been told by their parents, who were told by their parents, and so on so forth. Instead, we are now forced to create and justify our own beliefs rather than assume another person's or institution's to be true.

Now then, moral arguments against abortion emphasize the life of the unborn fetus, fertilized egg, "baby" or whatever you may call it. That is their strength, they feed on the morality, and the strong innate repulsion we have towards the harming of youth. I strongly implore the readers to cast a second doubt on this, as I will get into later within my own deliberations. However, for now, let us keep this in mind. Their argument is, admittedly very sound, and they believe that it is wrong for us to (partially) bring life into this world and then cancel it midway. At face value there is no counter to this argument, it is a solid argument. Murder is presumably wrong and immoral and so aborting of an unborn child should presumably be wrong as well. Especially since the child had done no wrong, and the only way to launch a somewhat successful campaign against this stance is by defending the autonomy of the woman. Proponents against abortion do this, and they may do it somewhat successfully, but nothing that can fully put down the irksome notion that we are depriving life to another living being. For this reason, and because of religion, the topic remains quite contentious even today. It also carries a sort of stigma and shame, especially if you live in an area that is not entirely supportive of abortions.

The moral foundations of the abortion argument serve as a seemingly insurmountable stronghold, and if you are free of dogmatic indoctrination, you may have noticed there is something wrong and unfortunate no matter which side you take. Say we are for abortions, then the mother is most pitiable as she is made to suffer through a pain no man would even be able to comprehend. However, if you are for abortions then the "baby" is to suffer a pitiable premature death.

To be a female, and even further, to be a mother is no easy feat. It is a process and a lifestyle that deprives one of their youths, their freedom, and for some, their joy. Nonetheless, parenthood is an amazing, and surely fulfilling role for many, and a perilous, frightening, and anxious ordeal for all. Before I begin going in depth, I believe it necessary that we speak of the pains and sufferings that women go through.

Pretend, if you are not one already, that you are a woman. You decide to have sex with a man, and you have discovered you are pregnant. Here is the first deliberation you must consider. You are about to have the child of a man, do you even like this man, do you wish to mother his child? There are those who say it matters not, but it matters very much. Because the man is free to go along, merry as one can ever be, and cheat, abandon, or do whatever he may please to the woman and still live a successful unhinged life. The man is free to have sex without worrying of getting pregnant, however the woman is not. The woman is the one who will have her life forever changed and burdened if stuck with a child, no amount of money can be taken from the man to remedy this. There are those, who repulsively say something like the women being a "slut" and should have not slept with the man. However, is this not wrong? The woman, who we presume to be equal to any man cannot enjoy the sexual comforts that her own body allows her, but the man can?

How many men would promise abstinence for the rest of their life and only have sex when they knew they think they have found the "one". It is a ridiculous notion; the question is not even worth asking. Is our society, our view, so cruel that we view women as *mere breeding cauldrons who exist for nothing else other than to give birth and satisfy men?* This, I find hard to swallow, and I feel obligated to prove otherwise. Women should surely be able to enjoy their right to sex as any other man. However, you may say, this is true, but she should just not get pregnant. Let us briefly assume this to be true, the women are at fault for their own downfall, and so she must give birth to the child if she is pregnant.

Though if we are to do this, let us look at the consequences, because even if the woman is at fault, surely, when making moral decisions we should look at the consequences. It would be ridiculous to sentence a man to death over mere fraud, or petty burglary, or some other small crime; even if someone has committed a moral wrong, if the punishment does not match the crime, then the punishment is unethical and wrong. Morality, ethics, and subsequently, justice, are not just about right and wrong, but also their consequences.

Chapter 6: The Multifaceted Risks of Pregnancies

Say the woman is forced to give birth. Now we are forcing upon her the physiological effects of labor which are, crankiness, mood swings, appetites, and the inability: to move around, drink, work, learn in school, and pay bills. Indeed, quite the list, and this is before the baby is even born. Let us also consider after birth. Mothers might have to rely and dependency on a possibly inadequate father, have poor job prospects, unfinished education, being forced to work an unwanted job with long hours, drastically increased financial burdens due to food, diapers, doctor bills, toys, clothing, day care, school, college funds, school trips, and more. Of course, if you are a single mother, you are also less attractive to most men on the romantic market, so romance, if you even have the time for it, is off the table, or challenging to say the least. This should not be surprising when you consider 66% of all remarriages, or couples living together, end up in divorce when children are involved (Step Family Foundation). You are also quite busy and stressed and the physiological changes to the female body after birth may make women not only physically less attractive but also emotionally and mentally unstable. If you were to forcefully impose any of the above to men, they would erupt in a violent protest virtually unmatched in all of history. Yet some of those same men propose it is moral to subject women to this, many, without even considering the permanent physical, emotional, and mental repercussions. Nor do they try to justify these repercussions outside of the common archetypes of, "sucks to be a woman," "shouldn't have gotten pregnant" and the more vulgar ones such as "slut," "whore," and more recently, "thot".

What if the woman is not ill-fated to be a single parent? Most of the above still applies, except now there is, arguably even more suffering. The man might have realized he has bitten off more than he can chew, and the lack of attention, sleep, and sex; and an increase in arguments, resentment, and child problems create a rift possibly leading to separation. After the first year of birth, a fifth of all marriages end in divorce; with women still suffering from much of the previous drawbacks from giving birth. Despite ~50% of marriages ending in divorce, let us say a divorce does not happen. In this case most of the above still applies, and hopefully either the man or woman are not impoverished or are able to escape poverty. However, many of the psychological, emotional, physical harm are essentially inescapable. Additionally, believe it or not the problem here should not be the risk of harm, but that this possible harm may now be forced onto a couple after a forced pregnancy.

The risks and tribulations do not stop there either, because upon giving birth not only do you crush most romantic encounters and what would otherwise be potential suitors, but prior to that you run a host of profoundly serious conditions. There is the actual experience of giving birth itself, which is frankly, terrifying. Because of our large brains, we need large heads to encase those large brains and so women are tasked with the gargantuan task of giving birth to, what is essentially a giant football. Unfortunately, there is no hole quite large enough to squeeze such a colossal figure through without suffering the worst pains most people will ever be subjected to. If you have ever grimaced or flinched at the mere idea or sight of birth, then you ought to imagine the *actual* pain of mothers. It is no wonder women also run the risk of death when giving birth to their children. This risk of death, of course, is found in much higher rates among black women, as they are 3 times more likely to die from giving birth (The Centers of Disease Control and

Prevention, 2019). Then, after successfully giving birth, they suffer from hormonal imbalances, many women, around 1 in 7, also suffer from postpartum depression within the first year of pregnancy, and 70% - 80% suffer from the "baby blues" (Carberg, 2021). Which, if they are lucky can be short lived, or devastating *if even diagnosed*. Unfortunately, despite not having the choice to stop the pregnancy, they are of course still liable for any actions they do even when they are not in their ideal state of mind after giving birth. Feeling isolated, depressed, and having no feelings towards the baby, are all common symptoms. Child negligence, child manslaughter, and sometimes even murder can be among the most sorrowful of tales. In underserved communities and in cultures with a stigma towards mental illnesses and mental help, these are far less likely to be addressed.

As one can see, giving birth is clearly full of risks, who she happens to get pregnant with, the toll on her body, finances, and her future love life are all at risk, while men risk relatively little. It is not so simple as giving up a portion of your paycheck to support a child, you must give your blood, sweat, and your very soul in the upbringing of a child. Financial stress is only part of it, there are psychological, and physiological effects, and the lack of time for physical and mental wellness will only perpetuate these problems, especially in poorer populations. If you are not yet convinced, or believe single motherhood is not a likely occurrence, you ought to know that in recent years the percentage of black families that were single parent households has been around 55%-60%, and that for white families it is "only" ~25% (United States Census Bureau, 2020).

Not only do the parents tend to be unhappy in a single parent household, but the children do as well:

> Parental divorce/separation is associated with an increased risk for child and adolescent adjustment problems, including academic difficulties (e.g., lower grades and school dropout), disruptive behaviors (e.g., conduct and substance use problems), and depressed mood.

> Offspring of divorced/separated parents are also more likely to engage in risky sexual behavior, live in poverty, and experience their own family instability. Risk typically increases by a factor between 1.5 and 2. (D'Onofrio, 2019)

If a couple does not think they are ready for children, there is certainly a compelling and diverse array of arguments in favor of an abortion.

This is not fear mongering propaganda, this is the cold reality of the country, of the world we live in, and that which we must face. No amount of child support can ever make up for the changes that take place because of pregnancy and furthermore through single motherhood. For centuries, we, the men, have pretended, or have just been oblivious to the fact that women enjoy sex just as much as we do. The only difference is that they get pregnant, and we do not. There is clearly a lack of empathy and care for women. The fact that the southern and most rural states who are proponents of Republican led efforts to adopt abortion, also happen to have the highest rates of domestic abuse also bears a scary implication (World Population Review).

Chapter 7: Redefining the Morality of Murder

In the previous chapters we have discussed the arguments in favor and against abortion, as well as how the parents are rarely ever considered. However, in this chapter we will be disgusting on the morality of killing, how we use the word killing, and the inconsistencies and mistakes that befall us when using this term.

Firstly, let us touch upon the usage of language that proponents of pro-life use. They call the unborn lifeform, a "baby". They argue we are ending life, that we are killers, murderers, and other things. Let me ask you, unless we are conducting a late-term abortion, where the baby can to some degree; feel, think, and exert will, then what separates the baby from any other cell, tissue, or organ? It is a notion rarely ever asked, perhaps because of its bluntness, or maybe because I have portrayed it with extraordinarily little tact, but the question remains. What makes this fertilized egg so special? Even before then, what makes humans special? Why is killing wrong? I suppose this is the most fundamental problem. Why is killing wrong? Or rather, when is killing wrong? Self-defense, the defense of others, and killing for the greater good can justify some killings or murders, so this means there are exceptions, if there are exceptions that means killing is not inherently bad or evil, and that whether it is good or bad is dependent on the situation.

Some may ask, "How can you conclude that killing is not inherently wrong?" To those same people I ask, do you conclude that a doctor is always right regarding medicine, or that the medicine itself is always good, or that lying is always bad? Surely, just because someone is a doctor does not always mean he is the greatest of doctors, or that he is infallible. Likewise, just because medicine is called, "medicine" does not mean it is always in the best interests of the body. Lying and withholding of the truth is not always immoral and it is sometimes the right thing to do. My point is, that in this world there are absolutes, and things that are not absolute, or what are known as contingent, and the things that are contingent far outnumber the things that are absolute. On the surface we may entertain blanket coverage beliefs such as *all* Asians are good at math, minorities are *all* poor, and that blacks are *all* criminals, but who in their right mind would belief these to be absolute truths. Does anyone actually believe *all* blacks are criminals, that *all*

Asians are good at math, and that *all* minorities are poor? Would anyone, stake their life for a million dollars because these things are obvious, absolute truths in *all* cases? No, so why is it that we issue blanket statements that cover far more than they ought to, such as, *all* killings are bad? Furthermore, we are not even capable, as a society, of coming to a uniform conclusion that *all* killings are bad. Therefore, it should suffice to say that killing is not intrinsically bad, if it were, it would be bad no matter the situation, it would not depend on the context, and there are rarely things as absolute as this. The only things that are absolutely good or bad, are the concepts of good and bad themselves. Otherwise, we fall into the common trap of association. This trap often occurs when there is a strong correlation between an action or concept, and a word or definition. Killing has a strong correlation with immorality and the characterization of bad and evil, but this should never be confused or thought to be synonymous with immorality itself.

To those who do not understand and still ask, "why". The answer is mistakenly complex; as humans, and as logical beings we tend to use words, concepts, and definitions to substitute or bypass deliberation, or thought. The concept of killing is one of those words and concepts. Let me further explain if I ask you, "what is a triangle?" You likely will respond that it is a shape. However, you do not stop to think why the triangle is a shape, you just know that it is one, and likely know why it is a shape, but you do not go through the mental gymnastics as towards why it is defined as a shape every time the word triangle is mentioned. Triangles and shapes, however, are quite simple and so you would never confuse the two subjects. What I mean by this, is that you would not make the mistake of *saying a shape is a triangle, rather than saying a triangle is a shape.* There is a profound yet simple difference between the two. However, for more complex and abstract thoughts we make this mistake all the time. We mistake correlation for causation for the subtlest of things. This is what happens when we carelessly use a word to substitute an entire concept. Relating back to the matter of killing, killing is highly correlated with the concept of bad, evil, immoral, and other concepts. But it should not be forgotten that killing is its own distinct concept separate from other concepts. Killing, and why it is bad, cannot be defined by concepts such as bad, evil, or immoral, these are merely traits that killers *sometimes* possess.

If someone asks you, "why is killing illegal," you may respond with, "because it is wrong, immoral, or bad." However, when was the last time you have ever examined why killing is *actually* wrong or immoral?

This is a serious flaw in thinking and is one of the major flaws in common unexamined thought. You may think this to be of little consequence, but when a good portion of people believe the world consists of simple absolutes that are black and white it affects our knowledge and the laws which we create. How do I know this? Throughout history people have been silenced for not just knowing more but being able to prove what they know is true. To the person being challenged this is a direct challenge to their will, their world view, and to some, their purpose. So much so, that they will seek out anything to validate their crumbling vision regardless of whether it is valid or not. They are preoccupied with saving face and not looking like a fool. It is imperative that we not think of the world as simple as we would like it to be, but as complex as it actually is; and that it would be better to be a fool for a minute than a fall for a lifetime.

This starts with knowing why killing is bad, listing the reasons why, when, where, and then acknowledging when it is good. If we do this prior to the formation of our own morals, we will avoid falling into the trap of association. To further illustrate my point, we only need to look at the usage of language depending on which side of the abortion debate you are on. Anti-abortionists use the words "kill" because it is associated with the concept of bad and evil. Then, they use the word "baby" because babies are associated with goodness, purity, innocence, and an actual live baby. For uniformity and consistency, I also use the word "baby," but think about how the usage of these words frames those in favor of abortion. It sneaks pass the conscience and evokes feelings of discomfort even though the words are not at all what they portray. The "baby" that is in utero is not even classified as such, and it is nowhere near the true concept of an actual baby. Furthermore, a fetus' pain perception is different from grown humans. They are not fully developed, and they cannot feel pain the same as whether that be in intensity or type.

But still, why, and when is killing wrong? Is it because we are depriving another person of their life? However, does this mean killing a pig is wrong, a chicken, an ant, what about our skin cells? Aren't we depriving life all the same? Surely the immorality of killing goes far beyond this. What makes killing truly immoral? I will seek to answer this. Let us say killing is immoral when we deprive, against the will of another, their right to life, when they possess no reasonable threat to any other life, livelihood, or property, and when to not kill is reasonable and possible for the person who possesses the opportunity to do so; lastly when it causes suffering, unreasonably, or unfairly to the person being killed or to those who would mourn for them.

For now, let us take this definition as is, others may add on to it, but I believe this to be sufficient for the purposes of this book. With this understanding of the immorality of killing, killing is immoral if the person possesses no reasonable threat to others and the environment around it. This means if the person or life form being killed has the potential to harm or destroy another's valuables; whether that be life or livelihood, then the killer is justified. If the person being killed is made to suffer when the suffering can be avoided without do something unreasonably difficult, or when the death of that person would cause suffering to those around him when it could have been avoided. Lastly, when it is done without the consent or will of the life form being killed, assuming it has abided by the rules set prior.

Chapter 8: Sentience & Morality

When speaking of the immorality of killing we should emphasize the being's will. The thing being killed must have a will, it must be sentient, it must be capable of feeling, suffering, and other like concepts for the killing to be immoral. The only way we can say the killing is immoral is if the killer takes pleasure in the feeling of killing. However, in this case we ought to say that the *killer is immoral, not the killing*, but it would rarely, if ever, be the case that someone finds stepping on ants, let alone abortions, pleasurable; and thus immoral.

If I were to throw water on a fire, I am not killing it, the fire was never alive to begin with. However, let us entertain this idea for a moment, let us say the fire is alive, it still would not be immoral, the fire has no will of its own. If fires were living, you may retort, "this is not so, the fire wishes to burn so that it may grow bigger and stronger and give birth to smaller fires". However, the fire is not capable of suffering, and even if it were, the fire does this at the detriment to its environment and the living things that it inhabits. So, even if you were to go out of your way to create a living fire, you still possess the right to extinguish it for the reasons prior. Clearly, "killing" this fire is not immoral. What makes killing humans wrong then, is not the fact that they are "humans", but it is because of the sentient quality they possess. Sentient beings that possess morality recognize and appreciate beings that share these similarities, and as a result we refrain from killing one another. On the contrary, we delight in the presence of each other, thus our natural curiosity towards intelligent life on earth and in space.

This is an indisputable fact, if not, then how else can we explain our persistent relationships with cats and especially dogs? Not only domestic animals such as these, but dolphins, orcas, parrots, apes and other highly intelligent, or sentient beings of the like? We feel next to nothing when we step on grass, or pull up roots of a plant or weed, no one cries of the immorality when we kill these or the bugs that call these vegetations their home. Therefore, it must be because of the sentient quality. It should be becoming obvious, regarding abortion, where my argument lies.

For much of the pregnancy the "baby" possesses no intelligence, no feelings, no heart, and certainly no sentience. To put it bluntly, I fail to see any difference between the "baby" and any other non-sentient life, or bodily organ. Also, take care to emphasize "of the body" because the "baby" does not even possess its own body. To say it does, would be as ridiculous as saying the heart, the liver, the intestines, possess their own body as well. Why? Well, does the "baby" not follow along with the biological intentions of the body? Does it not go to whichever orifices that the body allows it to? Remember this "baby" does not possess the will or sentience to ask the mother for permission. Ironically, in the earliest stages of pregnancy, the mother's immune system attacks the "baby" mistaking it for a foreign invader until the biological processes that govern the mother's body allows it to continue existing. Unfortunately, there is no way for the fertilized egg to get its mothers' verbal mutual consent, and humans have limited control over their inner biological functions, and so anti-abortionists would propose that the pregnancy itself should constitute as some form of consent because the mother "let it happen". As if when a person is sick or the body has a dramatic allergy response the patient in question just, "let it happen" why didn't they just take control over their cells and body parts if they did not want this? This is of course, absurdity, yet proponents of "pro-life" believe that abortions are immoral, and it certainly feels like they possess a compelling case. However, did we not go over the amount of suffering the parents, especially the mother, goes through? Why is it that we wait for the "baby" to near the development of personhood and then say it is immoral? How can an action be immoral if it is done to a living thing that causes, or will cause significant harm to them and possesses little to no sentience?

Here is where another problem in the "pro-life" argument lies. It is argued that abortions are wrong because they kill the baby or deprive life, but not all life is equal, sentient life clearly has more value, and I have gone over why this is evidently so. Since this is the case, why are we waiting for the being to develop sentience so only then the act of abortions will be immoral, and so that now at least, two people, the parents, suffer from the unwanted pregnancy and suffering then, now, and in the future, when they ought to have been able to avoid all of it. You cannot be immoral to something that does not possess sentience, will, or even existence! You may be able to think in an immoral or sadistic manner, such as how a deranged person might take pleasure and delight from stepping on or torturing insects, but if a person steps on an insect within their home they certainly are not immoral, while the former certainly might be.

There are some that might argue the "baby" has a biological will, or instinct to multiply its cells so that it may acquire sentience, I answer, this does not matter. The "baby" is not capable of feeling pain, and its biological instinct is something all animals and cells share, yet we kill cellular structures, in the billions, daily. The parents, however, can feel pain and suffering, it is better to alleviate their pain and suffering, then to wait for something to be able to develop the feeling of pain and supersede the parents' rights to avoid pain. Had we applied this logic to anything else, we would call the speaker mad. How ridiculous does it sound to say that we ought not to issue the death sentence to a man who has done wrong because he could have a child and it would be cruel to deprive existence to that child. Or that we should not lower the population of grizzly bears in an area, because it would be immoral to deprive their future offspring of their potential life; even if that meant causing the people and the environment around them to suffer. There are only two points in time in which we feel nothing, are nothing, and are entitled to nothing. One is before conception, before sentience, before will, or whatever you may call this state, and the latter is after death; if any person dares to claim he could feel when he has yet to even exist, in early days of pregnancy, or after death (an impossibility) then they are lying.

Chapter 9: Late-Term Abortions, Can They Ever be Justified?

What cannot be easily justified are the abortions of "babies" once they can feel pain, and more importantly, when they can be born, or are near this point. It is not that this cannot be justified, but it is because it is not clear when compared to an early fetus that is further back in a pregnancy. Again, we should take into consideration the parents and their own pain and sufferings prior, during, and after the birth. However, in this situation there is a tremendously large barrier that we must cross over.

This barrier is partially because the baby is now sentient, but mainly because the mother had several months prior to have an abortion. It would be either negligent, immoral, or cruel to wait for something to become sentient before depriving it of life, rather than depriving it of life before it has become sentient. It is far more reasonable and normal to discard of an egg, rather than to wait for it to hatch and then discard of it. Clearly the situation is different from the one before, and we ought to use a separate set of reasons to justify a late-term abortion if it is even possible to justify it at all.

Starting from almost nothing, one thing we do know is the suffering the parents go through, all humans are fallible, and there is room for mistake. However, when their mistake cost the life of another sentient's life or suffering, we ought to give some oversight. So then, in which cases is the mother justified in a late term abortion? I believe when she was unable to give consent. If a woman were to be raped, she has refused consent to the conception of the baby at least twice. One was when she refused or was not capable of giving consent to the rape. Second, which may be contingent on the woman, was when she reported she was raped. Third was when she explicitly expressed that she did not want the child. It is important for us to understand the nature of such a sensitive topic. The baby is not at fault, and the mother is not at fault, but there are some who will say that life must be preserved at all costs. Again, this is a personal or religious ideal, and the mother, or anyone else in the world for that matter, would not be obligated to sacrifice themselves for another, let alone an unwanted unborn child that is the result of the most heinous and traumatizing of crimes. If we are to say this is just, then we must imprison and fine those who do not sacrifice their lives for children in masse, because surely the children born are just as valuable if not more than those in utero. Therefore, we ought to do the morally right thing and imprison these adults, right? This is nonsense, we cannot hold people accountable for things that they are not, within the bounds of reason, responsible for. Therefore, there ought to be some room for leniency in a late term pregnancy abortion if it was a result of rape. Some may say that, how can a woman not know she is pregnant several months in? Although rare, it is very possible (Teicher, 2013), and contingencies like these present further challenges that I will address it shortly.

Since we now know consent is one of the conditions allowing for late term abortions, then let us shift our focus to pregnancies in under-age girls. Females who are underage, according to our law and society, are not capable of giving consent, or their consent is not sufficient because they are not yet mature enough to make good decisions. Since this is the case, the answer should be incredibly simple; late-term abortions should be permissible in pregnancies in which the mother is an under-age girl.

However, what if there is a conflict between the parents and the child. Suppose that the young girl wants to keep the baby, and parents wish to abort it. Also consider the opposite, what if the young girl wishes to abort the baby and the parents wish to keep it. Is there a difference between these two situations, should the answer depend? This is among the more thought-provoking hypotheticals, but I believe, if we are to assume and uphold that woman are more than simple baby cauldrons and tools for sexual pleasure, then we must give the right to choose to the underage girl, regardless of the parents' input. Even though the parents have custody of the child, and give consent and take responsibility for most actions of the child, it is important to realize, this is within the minority of things that parents have no say in. Parents have no right to choose who their children have sex with, who they love, nor can they force them to work a part time job. Anything that is permanent, life-altering, or with serious effects, needs either the consent of the child in addition to that of the parents, or just the consent of the child. It would be incredibly immoral to propose that children have no say in a decision of this magnitude.

However, what of the case in which the teen wants to keep the child, and the parents wish to abort it? The parents are still responsible for the child, but now should they be expected to be responsible for another child as well? It is here where things truly conflict. We presume that parents are mostly responsible for the actions of a child, and the child too, to a lesser extent. However, this is within reason of course. Which is to say, if a child commits murder or rape the parents would not go to jail, at most they may pay a fine in civil court, but they would never be sent to jail for a crime they did not commit. However, if the young girl wishes to keep the child it is her own body, and it should remain her right to choose, even if she is quite young. Then, what is the right answer?

In my own thoughts I found that the young girl ought to be able to keep the child, under some limitations. If the young girl decides to forfeit her right to an abortion, and the parents refuse to take in the baby, then the baby ought to be sent to foster care, or temporarily fall under the custody of another trusted party until she is legally able to assume legal custody of the child. This is, what I believe the fairest compromise, as all parties get at least partially satisfied. I also believe the father, or the father's family if the father is under-age, should first give up custody of the baby if the mother, or her family deny custody; before sending the baby off to a third party. As the parents of the child, they ought to have the primary right to custody before any other party can be involved. With grandparents and close relatives being secondary in priority, while friends and third-party caregivers being tertiary.

I propose another interesting scenario, one in which the father is well under-age, and the mother is of age. In this case, should the mother forfeit her right to an abortion, the father, or his parents should once again be given the opportunity to take custody of the child, but it ought not to be mandatory for either the father or his parents. The mother, of course, cannot take custody of the child as pedophilia is a crime and she would be serving a lengthy prison sentence.

In cases where there is no access to an abortion for an extended period, is another situation where abortions are justified. In some cases, some women may not have the resources, whether that be because of location or financial resources, to seek an abortion. It was only recently Mexico legalized abortions, but what if they did not? What if a family immigrating to the United States sought an abortion and could only get one after they arrived in America? This is yet another challenging answer. However, I do believe that a late term abortion could be justified because they were not capable of denying consent to the pregnancy at the time they were in Mexico.

Chapter 10: Ethics and More

Some criticism and concern may arise as it could be argued that in many cases my views are unfair or result in a sad ending for the child to be, however, there is a stronger argument for that of the parents. Even in the late term abortions the child is only scarcely capable, if at all capable, of expressing will, and whether they can feel pain or not is debatable. Furthermore, it is wrong to force one person to suffer for another, even if that person were at fault.

Imagine a heinous serial killer brutally rapes and murders a loved one, and then the response of an individual related to the loved one is to seek vengeance by harming a loved one belonging to the killer. So, this individual sets out to do so, and takes the killer's loved one hostage, and tells the police to trade the serial killer for the innocent hostage. What do you suppose the police should do? Also, what would you like the police to do? Keep in mind these two things are separate. One is to do with ethics, and the other to do with morality, and is the subject of this chapter.

Regardless of your answer, most, if not all modern governments would refuse to give up the serial killer. The only way the serial killer would even be near the crime scene of the hostage is if the serial killer agreed to a deal with the police. The reason I mention this, is because I want to emphasize that even if we assume it is morally right to have the killer atone by trading him for an innocent hostage, it would still be wrong to do so because we do not hold others accountable for the actions of others; even if that other person is the most detestable of humans and the progenitor of the problem; it is unethical.

If this example is to abstract, then, imagine there is an incident in which person 'A' incidentally leads to person 'B' developing kidney failure either on purpose or by accident. Should person 'A' be legally forced to offer their kidney if they're a match? No, this would be unethical. Thus, it would be wrong to force a mother to follow through on a pregnancy, even if she is at fault. There is no instance in our society or laws in which we force others to atone for their actions by having them sacrifice their lives, livelihood, or parts of their body for another. If nothing else, the laws and ethics we abide by ought to be consistent and evenly applied; what is their purpose otherwise?

Chapter 11: Combining Morality, Ethics, and Law

If it has not been challenging enough, we must also consider how morality, ethics, and law all play their roles in our societies and culture. Up until now we have only discussed the morality of abortions and have touched on ethics. Specifically, regarding abortion, there have been moral appeals, but now we will begin to discuss the ethical and legal ramifications of abortions.

In any given society, but particularly a democratic one, there are citizens, these citizens possess opinions, morals, and their own knowledge and understanding that serve as the basis for these opinions and morals. However, society does not run merely on morals, because morality is a subjective, and quite frankly, an abstract concept altogether. In a western society that emphasizes freedoms, such as in America, we ought to develop a higher standard of morality, one that is more uniform and universal. The main problem with morals is that they are not uniform and are dependent on cultures, ethnicity, location, education, and life experience. Yet, it is undeniable that in most cases; fighting, theft, and murder are all wrong. These common actions which we agree to be wrong are not just immoral, but unethical. Unlike morals, ethics is composed of a collective understanding of things that are moral and immoral. We all can agree that theft is wrong, and we all can agree that no person would want to have it done unto them, to protect ourselves we outlaw these obviously immoral actions. Through this we can conclude that any unjustified act of theft, murder, fraud, and the like all share something in common. That is, they cause harm to others who have not done wrong, as a society we unanimously agree this is wrong, and so it comprises part of our ethical code. Keep in mind that we are also a westernized culture; we emphasize freedoms like speech, expression, and various other constitutional rights. These are all part of our ethical principles.

As autonomous, or sentient beings, we also respect each other's autonomy and sentience, and so we understand consent is an important thing. Any actions which take away a person's right to life, liberty, or pursuit of happiness are also considered unethical. Also, a person who is not able to give consent ought not to be held responsible unless unreasonably negligent.

As a basic synopsis, we can say anything that causes unjustified harm, bypasses our consent, restricts our personal freedom, or restricts our happiness, or pursuit thereof is unethical. We have a right to all these things, granted we do not harm others to achieve them.

As a society we can agree that these are good ethical principles to abide by, and so anything that contradicts these ethical guidelines are unethical. You may believe this sounds synonymous with morality, but it is not. If a man were to kill another man out of cold blood, and then drops his weapon, he possesses no credible harm, however, many will feel that it would be justified for a family member of the victim to shoot the killer at once. They would argue they have a right to do so, and to say they are a bad or immoral person for doing so would not necessarily be true. However, according to our ethical guidelines this is wrong. The purpose of ethics is not to hold people accountable; it is to protect people and guide every person and institution on a generally agreeable moral set of codes. Also, if morality and ethics were the same things such as swearing, not saying, "bless you" after someone sneezes, or not saying a simple, "thank you" would become ethical issues. What may be considered moral in one situation may not be considered ethical in another, and vice versa.

Ethics serve as a good foundation for law. They are not the same, but they serve as a strong starting point. If something is unethical it is far more likely to be illegal. However, ethics and law, while strongly connected, are not the same. One way to envision this interconnectedness is through a hierarchy of relationships. Morality considers the person and the situation, ethics considers the society, and the law considers the outcome and their practical and applied effects. Morals and ethics hold a special relationship in which they affect one another, meanwhile, morality and law are indirectly linked but not as strongly as the link between ethics and law. Morality leads to ethics, and then ethics to law, but morality and ethics can also lead to one another.

One prime example of this is through the history and development of America. When Europe first colonized America they enslaved, raped, and colonized many lands. However, when the new American colonists living in the colonies opposed British taxation and other tyrannical actions, they portrayed the British government as unethical evildoers defying the common liberties and rights that men ought to have. It is ironic how it was only when they felt they were the subjects of tyranny that they called the government immoral and tyrannical. Whatever the case, it resulted in a new country, The United States of America, and this country was built emphasizing the ethical guidelines that Britain refused us. This is of relevance because the very ethics they upheld then, were incompatible and inconsistent with the morality of slavery and women's rights back then. Also, once again, during child labor and the industrial revolution, and then once more when the rest of Europe realized this too and renounced ownership of their colonies, then it was decided the use of some weapons in war were unethical as well, then once more during the civil rights era, women suffrage, and then recently with LGBTQ+ rights. For how long will humanity slowly correct its morality so that it may finally fall in line with our ethics? I cannot answer this, however, morality and laws take time to catch up with the ethics that guide them, and the common legalization of abortions in the western world remain consistent with our ethics. While morality lags furthest behind even when laws and ethics encourage otherwise, it too will eventually fall in line. Slavery has long been outlawed but rampant racism has only begun to falter in recent decades. It is my belief that just as we look down on the proponents of racism and segregation now, future generations will look down on those against abortion.

Chapter 12: Liberties and the Practical Implications of Abortions

I consider it our duty as citizens to understand the nuances of morality, ethics, and law. We all wish for the betterment and development of our society; however, when part or all a country is just insisting that their own ideas be put into law without any care for the ramifications, this becomes a problem. If there can be no consensus on whether an issue is ethical or not, then there should not be any law prohibiting it. If the continuation or the discontinuation of an action reduces harm and suffering without unreasonably infringing upon our rights and ethics, then it ought to be a law. If nothing can be deduced there ought to be nothing done until we can make a conclusion. This means that, regarding abortions, if no consensus can be reached, we should not try to make laws that restrict freedom.

If we were to allow the government to forbid abortions, then why should we not outlaw sex changes, hormones that induce sterility, and other drugs that reduce reproductive success? Is the unnecessary destruction of sperm and egg cells within the body not count, or is there some magic rule that makes the union of sperm and egg cells intrinsically more special? Regardless, it is strange that so many people care about what is going on in the body of someone else, if they do not like it, they must simply commit to not doing it themselves. This is the very basis of a free society; we do not force people to do things that they do not like when it does not harm those around them. Again, quite ironically, many of the proponents of abortion also believe that guns ought not to be restricted in their availability for purchase or in the types that are available for purchase. It is interesting how America has officially crossed the threshold in which over 50% of gun deaths are not a result of violent crime, but of accidental deaths. Whether that be by being overly vigilant and paranoid resulting in accidentally shooting an innocent person, or the gun accidentally going off, 50% of gun deaths are accidental. Not to mention the other half which have destroyed communities with crime, poverty, gangs, and school shootings. Yet guns are here to stay.

At this point, it might seem that my ideas are just the standard American liberal ideology that detests guns and supports abortions, but this is not the case. Rather, guns are proof that some liberties that we are afforded have drawbacks, some sort of sacrifice, and that it is unavoidable. We cannot have freedom of speech without being able to swear and yell slurs at people, we cannot have freedom of religion without having those that believe in no religion, Satan, or having arguments about religion. We cannot have the right to bear arms without incidents in which people use those arms to harm one another. Whether, according to the third amendment, we have this right at all is another matter, as its wording is confusing at best. But the opposite holds true as well, when we forfeit our right to speech during times of war, we become more united and secure. Whether we gain or forfeit any rights there is always an exchange of some sorts.

Yes, we undoubtedly lose something no matter what we do. Does this mean we ought to do nothing at all? No, we ought to look, examine the facts, history, and all that is available to us. We live in a world with plentiful amounts of data, and we do not need to look hard to find much evidence. One of the places we can look to is back into the past during prohibition which took place from 1920-1933. During prohibition alcohol became illegal, but as a result crime flourished, alcohol became a sought commodity that served as a major source of revenue for organized crime syndicates (Bynum, 1987). Furthermore, it was completely unregulated, and dangerous. Clearly moonshine made in a person's bathtub is not as safe as government regulated, factory made liquor. Do I believe that criminalizing abortions will lead to the second coming of the Italian mafia? No, I doubt it, but if someone wanted to get an abortion, who could stop them? What is to stop a family in Texas from taking a trip to Mexico where abortions are now legal? Or worse, what is to stop a mother from overdosing on alcohol or some other drugs in hopes of killing the child, or at best, giving birth to one with serious defects. A law that restricts freedoms, and changes nothing in the world of those who support it, except for a small temporary ego boost, is pointless.

Say we outlaw abortions nationwide, those who support abortions lose out, those who do not support abortions gain nothing but a small ego boost. However, what if abortions remain legal? There is no women's right crisis, no restriction of rights, the people who do not support abortions still will not have abortions anyway. Regardless of what you do, those in favor of illegalizing abortions gain nothing out of this, it makes sense that if there is a sufficient reason to ban abortions, that it is not found here. Any attempt to illegalize abortions are a matter of personal and/or religious preference.

I have said it much earlier, but to advocate for an issue on religious grounds is immoral, not once, but thrice so. Once, because you are attempting to impose your religion on another. Twice, because in a secular country you are trying to advocate for laws that go against the agreed upon ethical principles. Thrice because you are using something (religion) that cannot be proved as the foundation to enact a massive change or for political gain.

Secondly, we are perpetuating the racial disparity between races and between genders. The rate of single motherhood could increase, and thus women, who have come extremely far meet another setback in their fight for equality. Black women suffer twice as much as not only are they much more likely to become single mothers but tend to be less financially privileged, and thus a new moral question arises. With the amount of suffering an abortion ban could bring, is there anyone who can live with themselves knowing they helped cause it? When mothers seek an abortion in an unhealthy way, whether that be some underground doctor or consumption of chemicals, it is the women, the minorities, and the children who will suffer the most. And those of color, will be most affected by any (organized) crime that could prey on their communities. Even if there would be no criminal activities taking place, education and financial stability remain a chief concern for women. Especially as women become increasingly more independent and empowered, being forced to give up their own livelihood that normally any man is privy to would be a great disservice to our country.

As enthusiastic and passionate as the people behind pro-life are, they rarely address the somber, but larger implications. They would prefer to skip right over it, but the most important part of any argument is not the proof in support of it, but the proof against it, and sometimes the lack thereof. We should remember the much larger repercussions that an abortion ban would bring us. Even if you remain unconvinced by the arguments presented thus far, you still ought to think about whether your beliefs remain consistent. Do you believe we ought to have abortions but not offer support for the struggling mothers? Or that we should remain content knowing many children in single parent families are more likely to engage in detrimental behaviors? I ask that we do not merely look at whatever affirms our existing views, but also look at what disproves them, and the larger implications that our beliefs would bring to society.

Contacting The Author

Thank you for reading this book!

The best way to reach out to me is through my e-mail Philodre@outlook.com

You can also follow me on twitter @philodre

You can e-mail me for whatever reason. Whether it be to thank, criticize, argue, ask questions, or point out errors and flaws within the book. All input is deeply valuable, and I thank you for any feedback. I especially welcome criticism!

References

Anderson Dave. "10 Reasons Abortion Should be Illegal." ListLand, 25 March 2015, https://www.listland.com/10-reasons-abortion-should-be-illegal/. Accessed 9 September 2021.

Black A. Dan, Kolesnikova Natalia, Sanders G. Seth, Lowell J. Taylor; Are Children "Normal"? The Review of Economics and Statistics 2013; 95 (1): 21–33. doi: https://doi.org/10.1162/REST_a_00257.

Bynum, Timothy. "Brief History of American Syndicate Crime (From Organized Crime in America" P 15-29, 1987.

Carberg Jenna, Langdon Kimberly. "Statistics of Postpartum Depression". Postpartumdepression.org, edited by Langdon Kimberly, https://www.postpartumdepression.org/resources/statistics/. Accessed 16 September 2021.

Centers for Disease Control and Prevention. "Racial and Ethnic Disparities Continue in Pregnancy-Related Deaths." 5 September 2019. Racial and Ethnic Disparities Continue in Pregnancy-Related Deaths | CDC Online Newsroom | CDC Accessed 9 September 2021.

Derbyshire SWG, Bockmann JC. J Med Ethics 2020;46:3–6.

D'Onofrio, Brian, and Robert Emery. "Parental divorce or separation and children's mental health." World psychiatry : official journal of the World Psychiatric Association (WPA) vol. 18,1 (2019): 100-101. doi:10.1002/wps.20590.

Guttmacher Institute. "U.S. Teenage Pregnancies, Births and Abortions: National and State Trends and Trends by Race and Ethnicity" January 2010, U.S. Teenage Pregnancies, Births and https://www.plannedparenthood.org/files/5114/0236/1424/USTPtrends.pdf. Accessed 12 September 2021.

Hassenfeld, N., Vander Ploeg, L. (2018, April 10). *Today, explained: What's my wage again?* [Audio podcast]

Livingston G, Cohn D'vera. "U.S. Birth Rate Falls to a Record Low; Decline Is Greatest Among Immigrants" Pew Research Center, 29 November 2012, https://www.pewresearch.org/social-trends/2012/11/29/u-s-birth-rate-falls-to-a-record-low-decline-is-greatest-among-immigrants/. Accessed 10 September 2021.

Michael F. Lovenheim, Kevin J. Mumford; Do Family Wealth Shocks Affect Fertility Choices? Evidence from the Housing Market.

The Review of Economics and Statistics 2013; 95 (2): 464–475. doi: https://doi.org/10.1162/REST_a_00266.

Schultz T Paul. "Fertility and Income" Yale University Discussion Paper 925, October 2005, http://elischolar.library.yale.edu/egcenter-discussion-paper-series/933. Accessed 10 September 2021.

Step Family Foundation. "Step Family Statistics." https://www.stepfamily.org/stepfamily-statistics.html. Accessed 16 September 2021.

Teicher G Jordan. "Surprised by the Stork" Slate, 17 June 2013, https://slate.com/technology/2013/06/unexpected-birth-how-can-a-woman-not-know-shes-pregnant-until-she-has-the-baby.html. Accessed 12 September 2021.

United States Census Bureau. "Historical Families Table" Table FM-2, 2020 https://www.census.gov/data/tables/time-series/demo/families/families.html. Accessed 16 September 2021.

World Population Review. "Domestic Violence by State 2021." https://worldpopulationreview.com/state-rankings/domestic-violence-by-state . Accessed 11 September 2021.

Made in the USA
Coppell, TX
04 October 2021